READ THIS ABC POETRY BOOK TO HELP YOUR CHILD LEARN THE ABCS

Read this ABC Poetry Book to Help Your Child Learn the ABCs

Walter the Educator

Silent King Books a WhichHead Imprint

Copyright © 2024 by Walter the Educator

All rights reserved. No part of this book may be reproduced in any manner whatsoever without written permission except in the case of brief quotations embodied in critical articles and reviews.

First Printing, 2024

Disclaimer
This book is a literary work; poems are not about specific persons, locations, situations, and/or circumstances unless mentioned in a historical context. This book is for entertainment and informational purposes only. The author and publisher offer this information without warranties expressed or implied. No matter the grounds, neither the author nor the publisher will be accountable for any losses, injuries, or other damages caused by the reader's use of this book. The use of this book acknowledges an understanding and acceptance of this disclaimer.

dedicated to the parents that care about education

LEARN THE ABCS

Amidst the azure skies, a whimsical ode unfolds,
A tale of letters, a symphony of stories to be told.

A

A is for the apple, so crimson and sweet

B

B blooms a butterfly, in the garden's heartbeat

c

C dances the cat, with a tail so fine

D

D delves into dreams, where stars entwine

E

E echoes an elephant, majestic and grand

F

F flits a feather, gracing the land

G

G giggles the goat, in the golden glade

H

H hums a hummingbird, in the sunlit cascade

I

I introduces the igloo, in the icy expanse

J

J jumps a joyful jackrabbit, leading the dance

K

K kicks a kite, soaring high above

L

L laughs a lion, with a mane to love

M

M murmurs a moonbeam, in the midnight sky

N

N nestles a nightingale, singing lullabies

O

O opens an ocean, vast and wide

P

P prances a pony, by the seaside

Q

Q quivers a quokka, so cute and small

R

R ripples a rainbow, captivating all

s

S skips a starfish, on the sandy shore

T

T twinkles a turtle, forevermore

U

U unveils the universe, in the cosmic sea

v

V ventures a voyage, wild and free

W weaves a web, spun by a spider

x

X marks a spot, like a treasure finder

y

Y yields a yawn, as the night draws near

Z

Z zooms a zephyr, whispering cheer

THE END

In this lexicon of letters, an alphabet's embrace,
A poetic expedition through time and space.

ABOUT THE AUTHOR

Walter the Educator is one of the pseudonyms for Walter Anderson. Formally educated in Chemistry, Business, and Education, he is an educator, an author, a diverse entrepreneur, and he is the son of a disabled war veteran. "Walter the Educator" shares his time between educating and creating. He holds interests and owns several creative projects that entertain, enlighten, enhance, and educate, hoping to inspire and motivate you.

Follow, find new works, and stay up to date
with Walter the Educator™
at WaltertheEducator.com

www.ingramcontent.com/pod-product-compliance
Lightning Source LLC
LaVergne TN
LVHW051923060526
838201LV00060B/4149